WISDOM OF
THE NETHERLANDS

compiled by:
Gerd de Ley

with illustrations by:
Will Berg

Uitgeverij Verba

www.uitgeverijverba.nl

Translations by Gerd de Ley and David Potter
© Citafor vzw, Antwerp
Copyright for this edition: Verba b.v.,
Ede, 2007
Distribution: RuitenbergBoek, Ede
NUR 730
ISBN 978-90-5513-774-9

It's never too late for the past to
become the present.
Gerrit Achterberg (1905-1962)
Poet

If death cannot catch you,
it sends a specialist.
Cor de Back (1940)
Aphorist

The most difficult art to master
is the measured art of doing
nothing.
Simon Carmiggelt (1913-1987)
Columnist

Everybody is always right
but the strongest is more right
than the others.
Peter Andriesse (1941)
Writer

Five million years ago an
anonymous ape crushed the skull
of another anonymous
ape with a sharp stone.
Man was born.
Battus (1935)
Writer, born Hugo Brandt Corstius

Happiness is to be able to eat a
pancake without having
toothache.
Belcampo (1902-1990)
Writer, born H.P. Schönfeld Wichers

He who dreams of being nothing, has no imagination.
Okke Jager (1928–1992)
TV preacher

You must marry young, before you start thinking about it.
Nescio (1882–1961)
Writer, born J.H.F. Grönloh

Little children are cute,
but do you have any idea where
those big bastards come from?
Simon Carmiggelt (1913-1987)
Columnist

The language of the heart
knows many dialects.
Nicolaas Beets (1814-1903)
Writer

He looks like a scholar;
maybe he owns a quotation book.
Sannah Edens (1967)
Linguist

Trees are the legs of the
landscape.
I.K. Bonset (1883-1931)
Artist and writer,
born C.E.M. Küpper,
a.k.a. Theo van Doesburg

You can't criticise the present without long experience of the past.
Wim de Bie (1939)
Comedian and columnist

It would have been better for some talents to remain hidden.
Cor de Jonge (1930)
Aphorist

There is no horse market
without a donkey.
Proverb

There is so much to be
appreciated about trees – they
never call you, neither do they
write you letters.
Pierre Janssen (1926)
Museum director, TV personality

The difference between friendship and love is that friendship can bear absence.
Arthur Japin (1956)
Novelist

Man is a sad mammal that combs its hair.
Cees Nooteboom (1933)
Novelist, travel writer and poet

Everything is a lot for him who
doesn't expect anything.
Jacques Bloem (1887-1966)
Poet

There are two kinds of pit bulls,
the real ones and the false ones.
The false ones are the real ones.
Fons Jansen (1925-1991)
Comedian

Realism? That which is
unimaginable is real.
Gerrit Komrij (1944)
Poet and essayist

John Strange, the lawyer,
decided that his epitaph should
read 'Here lies an honest lawyer'.
All the passers-by, when they
see it, would exclaim
'That's strange!'
F. Bordewijk (1884–1965)
Novelist

The nice thing between man and woman is that they don't understand anything about each other.
Godfried Bomans (1913–1971)
Humoristic writer

Wishes that are fulfilled can't be cherished any more.
Lennaert Nijgh (1945–2002)
Songwriter

How do I make a poem?
That is very simple: it's like a
rooster laying an egg.
Martinus Nijhoff (1894-1953)
Poet

Someone without enemies
has no opinions.
Marcel van Dam (1938)
Politician

Art is combining the ridiculous
with the sublime.
J.A. Deelder (1944)
Poet, writer and performer

Thinking of the one you love is
always much more fun than
really being together.
Joeki Broedelet (1903-1996)
Actress, mother of Remco Campert

Soccer is war.
Rinus Michels (1928–2005)
Football coach

Football is like electricity.
Two months without it and
people are ready for revolution.
Freek de Jonge (1944)
Comedian

Hunger and pride are rarely
compatible.
Bob den Uyl (1930–1992)
Writer

There has never has been any
proof that there is any
connection between the girth
of your biceps and that of
your brain.
Midas Dekkers (1946)
Biologist and animal writer

Love costs nothing to get, but it is invaluable when you've got it.
Kees van Kooten (1941)
Comedian and columnist

Memories are a burden. They dominate the thoughts and fill the head.
Armando (1929)
Artist, writer and poet, born H.D. van Dodeweerd

Is your mirror also less beautiful
than 25 years ago?
Kadé Bruin (1915–1985)
Aphorist

If a computer catches a cold
the whole company is down.
Wiel Oehlen (1950)
Poet

The first victim of every war
is common sense.
A. den Doolaard (1901–1994)
Novelist, born Cornelis Spoelstra

It's easy to tell lies when
everyone trusts you.
Jeroen Brouwers (1940)
Novelist and essayist

They cannot go to war, because
they have to be home at six.
W.L. Brugsma (1922-1997)
Journalist

If brevity is the soul of wit
length must be the body of it.
John O'Mill (1915)
Humoristic poet,
born Jan van der Meulen

In most cases child protection is
nine months late.
Jan-Willem Overeem (1942–1979)
Poet

Some fathers like most other
people's daughters.
C. Buddingh' (1918–1985)
Poet, aphorist and diarist

The bible says: 'Drink your
wine with all your heart.'
But it doesn't say how quickly.
Simon Carmiggelt (1913–1987)
Columnist

Compassion is the worst enemy
of love.
Jan Wolkers (1925)
Novelist and artist

Poets lie the truth.
Bertus Aafjes (1914-1993)
Poet

Idealists keep their eyes firmly on the future. If they were to give just one glance at the past, they wouldn't be idealists anymore.
Eric van der Steen (1907-1985)
Novelist, poet and journalist, born Dick Zijlstra

Philosophy only serves to
contradict philosophy.
Willem Bilderdijk (1756-1831)
Poet

Money must roll, especially in
my direction.
Remco Campert (1929)
Poet and novelist

When you feel stressed
you should take a walk in a
beautiful autumn wood.
AND DON'T SHAKE
THE TREES!
Toon Verhoeven (1941)
Aphorist

Some people only marry just for
means of exchange.
Max de Jong (1917–1951)
Poet

When I look at the pictures of me in my puberty, I'm always glad I'm not my son.
Simon Carmiggelt (1913-1987)
Columnist

The frequent traveller can never keep his mouth shut about it.
Raoul Chapkis (1935)
Columnist,
born Hugo Brandt Corstius

The nicest way of cycling is with a person who regularly wants to rest.
Ben de Cocq (1945)
Journalist, born Wouter Klootwijk

Often I dream I am in hell. After waking up I realise – to my astonishment – that I am in Holland.
Jacob Israël de Haan (1881–1924)
Poet

A lot of people would have shortage of sleep if they couldn't go to the office during the day.
C. Buddingh' (1918-1985)
Poet, aphorist and diarist

The last man on earth sat in his room.
Someone knocked.
Jacques den Haan (1908-1982)
Essayist

Brainstorming is the privilege of
people who cannot afford to
think properly.
Gerrit Komrij (1944)
Poet and essayist

A stopped watch tells you more
about the time than a working
one.
Wim Hazeu (1940)
Biographer, essayist and poet

Once upon a time there was a
young man who married a very
ugly girl for her money.
When later he realized how
rich she was, he really started
to love her.
Gideon van Hasselt (1912-1993)
Poet, born Jaap Meijer

Silence is a hole in the noise.
Bert Schierbeek (1918-1996)
Poet

Luckily most people don't
notice that their marriage is bad.
Simon Carmiggelt (1913-1987)
Columnist

Do not rest on your laurels.
If you try, you will fall
through them.
Fie Carelsen (1890–1975)
Actress, born Sophia de Jong

I looked everywhere for peace
and quiet and the only place
I found it was with my book
in a little nook.
Thomas van Kempen (c.1379-1471)
Mystic, born Thomas Hemerken

Marriage is the tragic beginning
of a happy ending.
Havank (1904-1964)
Novelist, born Hans van der Kallen

Against the blue of the sky
every bird is black.
Jan Arends (1925-1974)
Novelist and poet

There is no other knowledge
than self-knowledge.
Carry van Bruggen (1881-1932)
Novelist, born Caroline de Haan,
sister of Jacob Israël de Haan

'I'll say no more', said the
drunkard, as he began to sing.
Herman Pieter de Boer (1928)
Writer and songwriter

Not every improvement
is a change.
Otto Dijk (1925-2004)
Playwright, born Ad. Odijk

Better to be homesick than in
Holland.
Leo Vroman (1915)
Poet

Better to be in Holland than
homesick.
Remco Campert (1929)
Poet and novelist

There is no finer art than modern art, except of course classic art.
Nico Scheepmaker (1930–1990)
Columnist and poet

Art critics are failed artists, like most artists.
Paul Citroen (1896–1983)
German-born painter

The walls are so thin that I
automatically take out a breast
when the neighbour's baby cries.
Adriaan Bontebal (1952)
Writer, born Adriaan van Rijn

It is around your fortieth year
that you cross over from the
sunny side of the street
and continue to walk
in the shade.
Maarten 't Hart (1944)
Novelist

If there was entertainment tax on feminism, our economical problems would be solved.
Gerrit Komrij (1944)
Poet and essayist

Noah is falsely represented as an animal lover. In fact he took all the cattle as provisions. How could he know the flood would end so early?
Jan Cremer (1940)
Novelist and painter

High trees catch a lot of fish.
Harry Mulisch (1927)
Novelist

Freedom of speech is only
interesting when you disagree
with each other.
Job Cohen (1947)
Politician

Hold on to the time
tomorrow you lose
another day.
Thera Coppens (1947)
Historian and writer

Only the wall that surrounds
friendship makes sense.
Wim Hazeu (1940)
Biographer, essayist and poet

People go fishing.
But what would they think if
fish went peopling?
Jules de Corte (1924-1996)
Singer-songwriter

In your youth you are dealt your
cards and you have to play them
for the rest of your life.
Jan de Hartog (1914-2002)
Novelist

Wheels are the thoughts of legs.
Harry Mulisch (1927)
Novelist

Marriage is a life insurance
for lazy women.
Renate Dorrestein (1954)
Writer

Most women are devoted to God when the devil doesn't want them anymore.
Gerrit Komrij (1944)
Poet and essayist

The best place to hide your heart is at the tip of your tongue. Nobody will be looking for it there.
H. Drion (1917–2004)
Jurist and poet

History is full of travellers
sitting in the wrong train.
H.W. von der Dunk (1928)
Historian

He who loves, lives and is afraid
of losing life.
Karel Eykman (1936)
Children writer and poet

Isn't everything illusion and is
illusion not everything?
Marcellus Emants (1848–1923)
Writer

People without humour
are mostly stupid.
Ton van Duinhoven (1921)
Actor

Once a loudmouth, always a loudmouth.
Gerrit Komrij (1944)
Poet and essayist

It's better to have a hundred failures than to do nothing.
Frederik van Eeden (1860-1932)
Novelist and poet

If eyes could yodel then the nose
would be a mountain.
Jan G. Elburg (1919-1992)
Poet

Our army is in fact very
democratic: every soldier is
considered equally stupid.
Rinus Ferdinandusse (1931)
Novelist and journalist

As long as there is no absolute
proof that I cannot do
something, there is a chance
I will be able to do it.
Rick de Leeuw (1960)
Rocksinger

To grow up is to be a able to be
a child without shame.
Jan Foudraine (1929)
Psychiatrist and author

Total abstainers are right,
but only drinkers know why.
Simon Carmiggelt (1913-1987)
Columnist

When wine is inside man,
wisdom gets a gentle smile.
Wina Born (1920-2001)
Cook book writer

Between the cradle
and the grave
a married man
only finds rest on the toilet.
Koos Speenhoff (1869-1945)
Singer-songwriter and poet

A meeting is where everybody
talks at the same time and
nobody listens.
Pieter Klaas Jagersma (1966)
Publicist

He who digs a hole
for someone else better doesn't
use a tea-spoon.
Miep Diekmann (1925)
Writer

Marriage - compared with
going to bed with each other,
this is a child's game.
J.A. Emmens (1924-1971)
Poet

Never trust a naked bank clerk.
Hans Ferrée (1932)
Advertiser and journalist

How wonderful it is that
nobody need wait a single
moment before starting to
improve the world.
Anne Frank (1929–1945)
Diarist

A love letter is sometimes better
than the lover.
Jan Slauerhoff (1898-1936)
Novelist and poet

When beauty fails, stupidity
makes its entrance.
Louis Ferron (1942-2005)
Novelist

When the enemy imposes rationing during wartime, it's called a war-crime. Now they do it voluntarily and call it a diet.
Jan Cremer (1940)
Novelist and painter

It is always dangerous to make confessions because of the domino effect.
Herman Franke (1948)
Novelist

Recently I saw somebody with green hair. Well, if I had green hair, I would paint it.
Herman Finkers (1954)
Comedian

Superstition is someone else's religion.
Jacques Bloem (1887-1966)
Poet

Why do people shake hands?
To show that you are not holding
a knife.
Such is the story of civilisation.
Dimitri Frenkel Frank (1928–1988)
Novelist, playwright and actor

You can do anything in a
caravan, but not at the same
time.
Seth Gaaikema (1939)
Comedian

If time is money, than eternity is
the hole in our purse.
Bergman (1921)
Poet, born Aart Kok

Only useless things
are indispensable.
Chris J. van Geel (1917–1974)
Poet

Have you noticed that we used to start off a telephone conversation with 'How are you?' and nowadays it's 'Where are you?'
Martin Veldhuis (1953)
Aphorist

If it's not real friendship, it won't last.
Hella S. Haasse (1918)
Novelist, born Hélène Serafia van Lelyveld

Writing is the recollection of
things that didn't happen.
Harry Mulisch (1927)
Novelist

The last years I hear more and
more about newspaperboys who
started out as millionnaires.
Eli Asser (1922)
Comedian and screenwriter

Life has but one purpose and
that is to learn not to fear death.
Joost Zwagerman (1963)
Novelist and essayist

Many friend, I grieve to see,
visit my bottles, instead of me.
John O'Mill (1915)
Humoristic poet,
born Jan van der Meulen

If you don't do anything,
everything will just happen.
Robert Anker (1946)
Novelist and poet

The lady barber asked me how I
would like my hair cut.
'Topless', I told her.
Herman Finkers (1954)
Comedian

Women cry more often than
men, but their tears contain
less salt.
Victor E. van Vriesland (1892-1974)
Poet

With a little patience you can
teach a grown-up a lot of tricks.
Madzy Ford (1922)
Novelist

The true seat of nobility is in the heart, not on a business card.
Arthur Japin (1956)
Novelist

Writing a letter to yourself makes more sense when you have the correct address.
Henk Bos (c. 1940)
Screenwriter and producer

Monkeys are much more
intelligent beings than human
beings.
Dick Hillenius (1927–1987)
Biologist, poet and essayist

Everything in life lasts long,
except life itself.
Jacques Bloem (1887–1966)
Poet

The nice thing about getting
older is that then every intelligent
person thinks: 'Ah, we're more
or less all bastards!'
Simon Carmiggelt (1913–1987)
Columnist

Lonely?
You know what lonely is?
An industrial zone on a Sunday.
Maria Goos (1956)
Playwright

He who hunts two hares
at once, catches neither.
Jacob Cats (1577-1660)
Poet and politician

If money were to rot as quickly
as milk or pears do, there
wouldn't be any problems.
Jan Eter (1935)
Columnist,
born Hugo Brandt Corstius

A pessimist is someone who
regrets what he is about to do.
J. Goudsblom (1932)
Sociologist

There are two kinds of people;
one kind does not exist.
Victor E. van Vriesland (1892-1974)
Poet

Scandal is one of the highest
forms of amusement.
Sonja Barend (1940)
TV personality

There are no intellectuals
anymore – only good Trivial
Pursuit players.
Ronald Giphart (1965)
Novelist

Silence is only golden,
when yours is the first voice
that breaks it.
Vincent Bijlo (1965)
Comedian

Lies are the penetrating oil of
human traffic.
Theo van Gogh (1957-2004)
Filmmaker and columnist

I dream my painting and then
paint my dream.
Vincent van Gogh (1853-1890)
Painter

Real heroes don't think.
Adriaan van der Veen
(1916-2003)
Novelist

A psychiatrist's interpretation of a hundredth birthday is as a manifestation of fear of death.
Toon Verhoeven (1941)
Aphorist

The purpose of schools is to teach us to forget.
Jan Hanlo (1912–1979)
Poet

Hope is the food of love.
Jacob Cats (1577–1660)
Poet and politician

A sex-shop is the only shop that
sells parts we already have.
Paul van Vliet (1935)
Comedian

If a robin pecks on your window, chances are it's a retarded sparrow.
Paul de Leeuw (1961)
TV-personality

Marriage is a school – a high school for patience.
Carel Vosmaer (1826–1888)

Poet

E-mailing leads to E-motions.
Bas van der Ven (1943)
Aphorist

You are really good when even
the worst you do is still good.
Jelle de Vries (1921-1999)
Composer

What annoys me about pessimists is that they are always right.
Cornelis Verhoeven (1928-2001)
Philosopher

The best part of time are the moments when it stands still.
J.W.F. Werumeus Buning (1891-1958)
Poet

Time is my enemy.
It takes away my lust for life and
in the long run, life itself.
Jacobus P. Bos (1943)
Writer

The cost of a Zoo ticket is high
due to increased wage bills.
By the way how much does a
hippopotamus earn these days?
Toon Verhoeven (1941)
Aphorist

It is unhealthy never to be sick.
Koos J. Versteeg (1907–c.1980)
Poet

High trees catch a lot of wind –
and also cast a long shadow.
Hans Warren (1921–2001)
Poet and diarist

A soldier is only a human being
cast in a certain mould.
Simon Vestdijk (1898–1971)
Novelist

My second wife ran off so fast
that she caught up with my first.
Lévi Weemoedt (1948)
Poet, born Izak J. van Wijk

To be in love is a kind of fever
on a higher level, that gives
existence suddenly a meaning.
Simon Carmiggelt (1913-1987)
Columnist

Jealousy is a monster capable of
consuming both partners.
Renate Rubinstein (1929-1990)
Essayist

Yes: the best answer to an indecent proposal.
Yvonne Kroonenberg (1950)
Writer

He who lives far from neighbours may safely praise himself.
Desiderius Erasmus (1469–1536)
Humanist

Only those who attempt the
absurd will achieve the
impossible.
M.C. Escher (1898–1972)
Artist

It is always nice when someone
drinks five times as much as you
and is still alive.
Monika Sauwer (1946)
Novelist, born Yolande Nusselder

The good old days – period when our ancestors had a very difficult time.
C. Buddingh' (1918–1985)
Poet, aphorist and diarist

The only 'Windows' that I have anything to do with are the ones that open in the summer and close in the winter.
Lévi Weemoedt (1948)
Poet, born Izak J. van Wijk

He who is rich has a gardener,
he who is poor has a little
garden.
Nico Scheepmaker (1930-1990)
Columnist and poet

Tourism: imagine a cornfield
that welcomes a plague of
grasshoppers.
Benno Barnard (1954)
Poet and essayist

When a pop group decides to make a come-back it is usually because they just received their tax bill.
Jan Blaaser (1922–1987)
Comedian

That which remains never returns.
Jan Eijkelboom (1926)
Poet

Those who are afraid of silence
have never read their own heart.
C.S. Adama van Scheltema
(1877–1924)
Poet

Theatre is illusion,
with a little help from magic.
Karin Bloemen (1960)
Singer

Even pigs smell good when they
use a deodorant.
Max Arab (1931)
Cartoonist,
born Evert Jan van den Vlekkert

A pound of feathers
does not fly
if there is no bird in it.
Bert Schierbeek (1918-1996)
Poet

Music completes what the word
couldn't express.
Lodewijk de Boer (1937-2004)
Playwright and musician

What a pity we cannot use our
future experiences to make our
present decisions.
K. Schippers (1936)
Writer, born Gerard Stigter

Your neighbour always seems to know how wrongly you do things, but on the other hand we know how wrong he is too.
Simon Carmiggelt (1913-1987)
Columnist

Is there life after death?
I think so, yes.
Still, I don't think I will experience it.
Wim T. Schippers (1942)
Artist and TV writer

The day is an appletree
but you have to pick the apples
yourself.
Toon Hermans (1916-2000)
Comedian

Now that I finally have the
money to buy an expensive dress,
it won't fit me anymore.
Annie M.G. Schmidt (1911-1995)
Writer

In the process of evolution
man is but a transient species.
There is still hope.
Toon Verhoeven (1941)
Aphorist

He who is lifted by dwarves
will never be far from the
ground.
Frans A. Janssen (1939)
Linguist

Electronic sound distortion
saved many lead singers.
Dimitri Frenkel Frank (1928-1988)
Novelist, playwright and actor

When you have a race with a
bull, try to stay behind him.
K.H. Veldhuis
Graphic

Even a radio is silence
when you switch it off.
J. Bernlef (1937)
Writer, born H.J. Marsman

It is true, I saw it in my own
dreams.
Herman van Veen (1945)
Comedian

You don't say more with more
words.
Bertus Aafjes (1914-1993)
Poet

One thing worse than jealous
women: jealous men.
Mies Bouwman (1929)
TV personality

Travel gives you the opportunity
to see yourself against different
backgrounds.
Jan Brokken (1949)
Novelist and essayist

Often something has to be done
before anything gets done.
Johan Cruijff (1947)
Football player and coach

A sociologist is someone who proves you that it will go dark when you switch off the light.
Jan Blokker (1927)
Journalist

If I were you, I would come back to me.
Marion Bloem (1952)
Novelist and painter

The best way to show your disagreement is with constant nods of approval.
Wouter Wytynck (1931)
Aphorist, born Chris F.J. Schriks

Love makes a big bed small.
F. Hellers (1936-1998)
Educationalist

Smoking is bad – especially for
the curtains.
Willem van Hanegem (1944)
Football player and coach

A fanatic is someone who
doubted and took a decision.
Godfried Bomans (1913–1971)
Humoristic writer

Marriage is adultery with your
legal wife.
Harry Mulisch (1927)
Novelist

In this world there is a woman
for every man... until his wife
finds out.
Max Tailleur (1908-1990)
Humorist

There is nothing more
insignificant than a man
and nothing better exists.
Hans Andreus (1926-1977)
Poet, born J.W. van der Zant

It would be nice
if Summer would fall
on a Sunday.
Gerard Brands (1934)
Poet, born Gerard Bron

The most beautiful sight
I know
are forty bottles
in a row.1413
Jan Boerstoel (1944)
Poet and songwriter

Living is just one way of losing
your hair.
A.F.Th. Van der Heijden (1951)
Novelist

The strength of a man is to see the pro or the contra; the strength of a woman is to be it.
Godfried Bomans (1913-1971)
Humoristic writer

Women walk slowly in order to make their beauty last longer.
Stef Bos (1961)
Singer-songwriter